Passion & Provocation

Passion & Provocation

Selected Poems
by
Judith Partelow

atmosphere press

Published by Atmosphere Press

ISBN 979-8-89132-179-3

Cover design by Ronaldo Alves
Cover photo by Nathan Butera

Atmospherepress.com

Dedicated to
Joan Graham
who encouraged my writing
for almost half a century.
I wish she were here to see this result.

Contents

LOVE'S DEMISE & OTHER LOSSES

MEMORIES

SENSE OF PLACE

SPIRITUAL CONTEMPLATIONS

TRIBUTES

THE BEGINNING

I stand naked before you
bearing no flag or cloth
of any color.
I have my so-called work
voluminous in measure
but in quality,
there's the rub.
Is it for my own pleasure
or true treasure?

I used to write

when the lump in my throat
hurt so much
it splattered ink
all over paper.

I haven't written for a long time
but suddenly life seems summed up
and my throat aches
it aches.

I am one of the women
you haven't read about before.
We never speak our insides out.
(We have too much to lose, or think we do.)

But you'll be reading all the stories anyhow
in one newspaper or another
over coffee.

For the silent women are clamoring to be heard
though you've never seen
a single, printed word.

At a Reading

Your Indian poet
and the rain
were just what I needed
to celebrate the end
of anonymity
and entertain
again
the hope of ink, dyed red
to drip a drop of life
upon the page.

Writers' Place

This is ours
this place where writers go
between the dusk and dawn
formulating lines
behind the eyes.

This is where we meet
on a precipice
overlooking mountains of space
dancing with our pens
in the spill of the moon.

My poet's heart believes
this company of dreamers
will chart a course
that those hereafter
will exclaim as truth;
the tests of time engrave,
no winds erase.

Poems

Great poems
like new lovers
lie on my pillow
promising to be there
in the morning
but they never are.

Old poems
annoy me
as old lovers
once fresh and full of promise
grew tired of rejection
and vanished.
A whiff of cologne
still lingering on the sheets.

Reading

under a yellow lamp
that sheds warm light
on my book
I sit in a cozy chair
reading
breathing softly

sounds of raindrops
on the windowpane
and pages turning

I could be Lincoln
or Edison
the Pope
a missionary
a farmer
an engineer
a fireman
a veterinarian
or anybody

who is lucky enough
to know how to read

but I'm just me
who has a grey day
and a cozy chair
in which to sit quietly
under warm light
turning pages

breathing softly
reading about
some other kind of life

Censure

They have not hung me
with the other poets
up against the wall
but the invitation opens
like a wide smile
and swallows me.

Words rise and burst about my head
filling me with trepidation, fear, and dread.

My fingers hold each other tensely
for they must be still.
In this darkness
I mustn't make a racket
scratching
with a feathered quill.

Written on behalf of all writers who are censored and persecuted for exposing tyrants.

DOMESTIC THEMES

These I see now, clear-eyed
no distraction.

Clear Eyes

Perhaps age grants sight

of sunsets more lovely
though there were always sunsets

of luscious scruffy bushes
washed in watercolor

of a tiny broken shell blown beneath a fence
once swelling on a wave

or the last rose
bending crippled on its stem.

These I see now, clear-eyed
no distraction.

I contemplate and sip each draft
to slake the thirst of youth in haste

who could not stop to quench or taste
in fitful quest for truth.

Quiet Pleasures

Watching cattails blowing in the breeze
Driving through autumn's blazing trees

Passing walls made with rocks and stones
Licking ice cream cones

Seeing a sunset anywhere
Washing my hands for prayer

Tasting rich coffee in a cup
Having my love there when I wake up

Reading in a comfy chair
Touching a newborn's hair

Taking a nap on a rainy day
Sculpting with clay

A handwritten letter addressed to me
Invited to a friend's for tea

Knitting a gift as a surprise
Looking into my dear's kind eyes

Showering with scented soap
Eating grilled cheese and tomato soup

Husband massaging my tired feet
Slipping between clean sheets
But of all life's quiet pleasures
by far the best
Nursing my babies at my breast

Motherhood

Under a long cotton nightgown
We have swept away a thousand nights
pinning a sap-sucking honeybee
against a naked thorn.

Women with cool ankles
leap across doorways
and bend above the cribs of time
to dribble blue ink inside a hollow well.

Moistened fingers clinging to our hair
play a fiddle-tune

an endless tune
we dance to all our lives.

The Sandbox

She inspects bugs
pushes pebbles between her toes
squeezes squishy mud
shifts shapes
giggles with playmates.

No idea of what's to come
as rainbows in her world
fracture
into viruses
choked dying oceans
polluted air
warring nations
bigotry
racism.

I envy her
wishing I didn't know
what she doesn't know
as she marvels at discovery.

But I must prevent her
before she collects
treasures she spies
on the beach:

colorful mini nips
cigarette butts
plastic straws
syringes
broken bottles
crushed cans.

Her first fascination
with her world
sullied
by those
who've forgotten.

Fingerprinting

Our fingerprints are on our children
the moment they're conceived
from our DNA and diet
to what we do or say.

Then after birth our views
our morals
our beliefs
and often what we wish they wouldn't learn

are stamped upon their thoughts
along the way.

They are fingerprinted by their friends
their teachers and the neighbors
salesmen, priests, or rabbis
television shows and films.

We have one chance
to fingerprint our children
with values
for their lives.

They cannot be erased
reconstructed or replaced.
Once imprinted in their minds
the fingerprints

will stay with them
a lifetime.

Parent Night

The ninth grade English teacher
has Siddhartha eyes
as he makes his case
on Parent Night
pounding soft chalky fingertips

emphasizing
punctuation
sentence structure
completed homework
punctuality.

We sit in students' desks
nodding, smiling
glancing at the clock
squirming like our children
listening for the bell.

Sandpipers

At eleven
my neighbor's twin granddaughters
look like sandpipers on the beach

    long thin legs
    making their way up
    to small slim bodies.

They dart back and forth
between sand and water
hopping and squawking

    digging and dipping
    about their own business
    like young birds.

Too soon they'll be aware
of how to roll an eye and hip
to attract their prey

    forgetting bird-like scavenging
    for other kinds of gatherings
    on the beach.

Anthology

I keep jars of multi-colored glass
found on scattered beaches where I walk

a collection of colors
the gathering of which
joins the jagged edges of the past
and holds them safely
in a bottle on my shelf.

Pieces of pottery intrigue most:
broken cups and saucers
dishes, and tureens

the wares of women spilling off the waves
faded patterns of a woman's dreams.

The crockery seized and smashed
that once was filled

then washed and wiped
and gently placed upon the board.

Tomato Plant

The harvest
of this summer's quarantine.
A tangible pleasure.

It's the first fruit I've grown
in my seventy years.

I cradle the pot like a baby
from porch to kitchen to capture the sun –
water and speak to it
with loving encouragement.

It listens and bears first red
then when there is no longer
ample sunshine to make it blush –
green tomatoes.
I pluck the largest
gracefully shaped tomatoes
to slice and fry
enhancing my dinner with luscious *umami*.
Some smaller ones line up
along my windowsill to ripen.
A pungent aroma rises from the leaves
when picked, as if to say, *ouch!*

It's grown tall over the summer
like schoolboys do.
It yields such delight
for most all my senses.

I wish I could hear it grow
in the silence of the night.

Last Summer's Flowers

Stripped bare
by winter's batter
last summer's flowers
provide the matter
for cradles
to hatch baby birds.

I watch the mothers snap
dry geranium stems
then methodically
transport them
to build their nests.

I'm glad I'm not
the type of gardener
to denude my flower boxes
at the end of summer.

I like spying on chipmunks
and squirrels
as they pick around
foraging for their winter stores.

Then, come spring
the robins and wrens
recycle what was last year's
feast for the eye
as scraps for practical use.

Birds giving thanks
for chaff from my garden.

Moments

Petals pressed between pages
weedy tendrils shifting in a breeze
kelp drying on dunes
bleached sheets hanging on a line
humpback whales rising

Vibrant kites against the sky
flaming autumn leaves
rocks dashed by angry waves
sun sinking behind mountain
paint speckled on a fence

Curls cascading down a child's cheek
smooth stones skimmed across a pond
saxophone's sultry moans
homeless man's coffee-stained shirt
scent of mother's lipstick

Damp monastery walls
light streaming through windows
handwashing in warm water
kneeling in penitence
counting beads through fingers

Wisps of cool, sweet air
bells calling to supper
boys shouting, *In a minute!*

Clearing the table
shaking out the tablecloth

Skylights

Huge snowflakes lick at my skylights
sliding down to the edge
like children on sleds.

I love these windows
that face the heavens
requiring me to look up
first thing each morning
and last thing each night
when the moon
captures my final resting thought.

They are the forecasters of my day.
They provide the hope that all will be well
for day after day
they patiently allow
the sun to enter
rain to pelter
wind to batter
snow to blanket.

But in the end
they provide clarity of vision
as my own light shines through them
into the world.

Kitchen Drawer

The spoons are lining up
small ones nesting in the large
forks cradled in their spot
butter knives aligned
the reckless clutter of another life
is gone

You bring order
practicality
virtue
form
and that which is
harmonious design
now the norm.

Reverie

At dawn he sits, gazing east
his dog-eared book face down
on the worn blue blanket covering his knees.

Tenderly, he sets his finger
to the cold light in the sash
tracing patterns formed by accumulation of
changing conditions between the panes –
recalling her;
remembering
when there was nothing to lament
but a windless day.

How would you like your eggs, dear? and
Put your slippers on, it's cold,
she'd said countless times
since they were wed.

Had he recognized the loving hands
or felt the comfort of her voice
with her steadfast dedication to his needs?

He smiles as the carefree boy
appears through the glass
pivoting on the rocks
skipping stones and sailing boats
salt and sand in his tousled hair;
rejoicing in the promise
sunrise
gleaming shells

slick moss between his toes
and undulating waves
could hold.

A fog-horn startles him awake.
Confused about the hour, day and place –
but the boy is gone, his sailboat on the shelf;
she is not here –
and there lies the book upon the braided rug
she made of scraps from her trove of aprons,
stockings, socks sewn together, she said,
to keep the chill off the floor.

Age

Day closes the door behind her.
Evening sits down at the table.

There's a hum you don't hear 'til it stops:

Dishes clicking off shelves
potatoes bubbling in the pot
cats circling their bowls
crossword clues, half-whispered
find a slot.

The daily news chatters
birds rustle in their cage
you chew what you are able
and turn the page.

LONGINGS

You see me as a small-town actress
caught up with big-time dreams
and you smile behind your tinted glasses
politely clapping to my screams.
This weaving that you see before you
this dancing for a throng
merely scrapes the surface
of the need to tell my song.

Siren

Cold droplets bead across my brow
in jeweled formation.
Heat.
Unseen blankets cover me.
Dry, moistless sucking in of air.
My fan cannot redeem me.

I shall associate our meeting
with these first heavy breaths
of heated summer-longing:

a touch of chill to cool
my sweating arms
my open thighs
my sultry swaying walk
my furtive, beckoning eyes.

June is heavy
with her burgeoning summer-child.
When she delivers
these days of languid tension
she will deliver us all
from temptation.

Connection

Two elements
electrically compatible
plug and socket

remain uncharged
indefinitely
without connection.

But in the course of events
if they make contact –
that current flowing through them

will send out
light, heat, a whirr, a buzz
until they are dissociated

by the wearing down of one
or unplugging
by the other.

Calypso Afternoon

Torrents of rain
shutter-beat the windowpane –
counterpoint to soft-sung song.

Smooth drink
smooth sound
smooth-skinned
smooth-boy –

she is strung across the bed
a well-tuned taut chord
waiting.

Tropical ma-an
pulsates to a calypso beat
with tropical wo-man
in syncopated rhythm

as heat in waves
crests then falls
on a rolling raft of linen sand.

Assignation

Wrists bent hard against pillows
glued to the phone
better to aim the breath
transcending doors, windows
and sail its arc to love's canal.

Communion with a long-distance lover.
Filling up the silence
in the lonely
sleepless night
before the dawn.

This niche we cull with our own hands
howls its spirit like a headstrong girl
who wasted and done
drips water like a fish wife
going out to market to advertise her wares.

But we have not breached the pass.
We have caught the plaintive tune
yet, strain to hear the words.
We have moistened up the seal
without compressing it.

We are holding on
on hold, for all the world
and choose to speak our silences
in muffled moans, or bits
of crumpled paper on the floor.

First Sight

My heart stopped
when our eyes first met.
Oh, my God,
I thought.
Here he is.

Handsome.
Virile.
Voice
to die for.
Damn.

I tried to remain
calm
poised
balanced
as my face flushed.

Then, just as the springboard
propelled me upwards
arching gracefully
on my toes
I took a dive.

There I was
bobbing underwater
gasping for air
when I realized
he was not alone.

What Is Not

Never has the lack of kisses
been much sweeter.
Unspoken language been so full of meaning.
The juice from berries not yet tasted
been this ripe and bursting with exotic flavor.
No sleepless nights more savored
for the want of dreaming.

Never such an unfamiliar face more welcome
than the sun in dreary winter.
Songs not sung heard running through
my quiet mind.
Words unexpressed so loudly
breaching stillness.
Or lightly touching fingers with more fire
than all their skin aligned.

The faintest smile never more desired
than brittle soil needs torrential rain.
Time and place have lost their implication.
That which is real but doesn't have a name.
No announcement is my latest information.
There's nothing that for now I can explain.

A Man Like You

Man
walking down the street
our glances meet then slide away
like partners in a dance.

I contemplate
your hot sweet lips along my naked back
your tongue lancing at my ears
your white teeth teasing
at my soft white breasts
your warm hands gliding down my legs
your lean hard body raging into mine.

I wonder who your woman is
and if she sees you as I do
all man and sensuality and promise.

Does she wrap her arms around you
each day begging you to stay?
Or does she send you out into the world
a beaten, broken remnant
of the boy she took and held
with long thin fingers
and tensed fervent thighs
until you succumbed
and gave yourself to her?

Who'd throw a man like you away?
I'd shake that woman and open up her eyes.
I'd tell her there are lonely girls out here like me

who'd gladly take a man like you
and passionately whisper
and laugh out heartily at foolish wives
who'd throw a man like you away.

There is the slightest trace
of smile on your face
as our bodies faintly signal an embrace
then turn the corner to our separate lives.

Morse Code

If glances were currency
I've spent a fortune on your face.
When I look into your eyes
my pulse begins to race.
I'm telegraphing all my thoughts
of love
and wish, My Love,
you'd telegraph a message
back to me.

I don't dare speak the words
for fear you'd laugh
and you probably won't guess
this is for you.

So, my love will have to come to you
in code.
Should I tap it on your window
tap it with my pen
or tap it with my spoon against a glass?

I would do it any way you want it
and if you understand
you could have this woman's heart
if you tapped a Morse code
back upon her hand.

Lilac Wine

I wish I could take your sweetness
add it to Lilac Wine
bottle it, cork it
and save it for the times
I need something magnificent
to appease my longing
for some moment of you.

But it would be gone too soon.
For with each glass I'd pour
I'd take just one more sip
and be worse than I am without you
even now, the empty bottle
leaving me in withdrawal
and no hope for a cure.

Love Quest

Need reached out for you
in early morning hours.
It curved around the closest legs
the nearest breath
in calm, emphatic quest

and burst
in resolute defiance
across the plains that separate
the road I'd travel in
to you.

The road I would
you'd travel
into me.

Safe Harbor

Are you so blinded
by my radiance
you must seek another harbor
while I beam like a lighthouse
to bring you safely
through the rock-strewn way
you are navigating?

I revolve like a beacon shining
washing with love
everything in my path.

But it is you they see
burning out of me.

Walking among the rhododendrons

Little lanes quietly winding
gave way to explosions of color
towering over us
as we walked among the rhododendrons.
Yet, in that riot of fragrant beauty
and mild threat of impending rain
there was a hush.

We slipped in and out of well-worn trails
marked with quiet conversation.
I snapped a photo of you, and you of me
under a rhododendron tree.
Your admission tag hung front and center
made you seem a marked deer
that would run if you were a different sort.
But you stand strong and tall
balanced evenly on your legs
smiling into the headlights
of my conspicuous love
with covert pain behind your eyes.

My picture reveals contentment, joy –
hip slung carelessly; shirt tied at the waist –
a casual come-hither pose
that can't seem to work its charm.

A small bench was our table
for the picnic lunch I made
marred somewhat by flour, freezer-burned
in the cornbread you tried

but failed to convince was okay.
I encouraged you to toss it away.
Oh, how I wish your hurting mind
could so easily be pitched into the pines!
But you are innately kind
disguising gallantly your turmoil
with a concentration like
the leaves and rocks bordering our path.

You kept on track, moving forward
holding gently my willing hand
and in the hush made me forget
your thoughts were somewhere
far away.

Uncommon Sense

We are
in the uncommon sense
lovers
in a truer form
than ever I have known.

If love is to be patient
if love is to be kind
if love is to ask little
yet persist with loving
when no hope waves its flag

then the manifestation of wanting
expressed in dull and constant ache
can only be and is
as water refines the rock.

Tire Tracks in the Driveway

I look down from my second-floor window
and see your tire tracks in the driveway

the ones you made that night
under the moonlight in your hasty retreat
after you held open your coat
so I could wrap my arms around your waist
while you kissed me; a warm kiss
that I repeated while holding your head against my face.

I wonder where you've gone
why you don't call, what I did, or said
to make you go?

Is it you who doesn't know
just how to love a woman
who could love you with all that you are
and despite anything?

Or is it me, who wanted to be there
inside your coat with you
to press my breath into yours
too eagerly responsive
that drove you, made you drive away
leaving the imprint of your tires
as a trace of your embrace?

Uncertainty

It would be so much easier
if he'd just tell you
he didn't want to see you anymore

but this uncertainty
the not being sure
churns your stomach into sour milk.

You want him to call so that
you will not answer the phone.
That'll show him how angry you are –
how you are not someone to be toyed with.

You made the mistake
of telling him you loved him.
At the time it seemed so mutual
so safe and lasting.

But now he isn't calling
texting
or emailing
not to mention using snail mail

and you go through all the excuses possible
to justify his behavior and try to be patient
until finally you realize he's just a jerk
and you really don't give a damn anymore.

Then he calls.

That One

At my work in the surgical unit
I see couples
lots of couples.
Couples who've been together for a long time
or maybe not so long.

I observe little things:
signs, and touches, jokes, and laughter;
annoyances, curtness, disparagement.

I make note of the ones I want
and don't want for my life.
I see men who can't get away too soon
when dropping off their wives for surgery.

I see the men who pace and worry
and can't wait to go in to see their wives
before and after major and sometimes very minor surgeries.
I feel envious when a man is sweet, tender, caring
and doesn't seem to notice anyone else
but the woman he is with.

I want that.
I want that man who can see only me –
who sees into me
who sees with me
confides in me
rejoices with me
cries with me.

I want those fingers intertwined with mine
that love-breath on my face
that gentle pressure where I hurt
those eyes that search my face for how I feel.

I want that for me.
That man. That one.
That one.

LOVE

Give me music
grow a perfect rose
read with me in bed
write in tender prose
talk with me 'til morning
feed me toast and tea.
These are all the gifts I need
as long as you love me.

Train Story

She is heavy and homely.
They don't necessarily go together
but in this case, they do.

He is shorter than she
thin, Indian.
His brown head rests against
her white bosom
as they sleep together on the train.

They are an item.
They have been traveling together
I have noticed
for a year.

In winter, with scarves and hat
and large wool coat
she saves a seat for him.
She looks around nervously
if he doesn't come and
she saves her smiles just for him.

When he arrives
he looks so businesslike
in his business suit
although his boyish build
defies such description.

I have never seen them talking.
They make little signs and signals
that betray their love.

It is so touching, so heartening
to see these two
this unlikely pair
display affection
which they hold so dear
so openly

by sleeping on each other's shoulders
Manhattan to Stamford
on the New Haven line.

After "Rain Effect" by Mary Ruefle

A bride and a groom sitting in an open buggy
in the downpour saturating them
and their guests who race
to the reception underneath the tent
huddling in the center of the canvas
avoiding the rain blowing in
hoping for the rain to stop
and for the music to begin.
Fathers and mothers
uncles, nieces, aunts
best-man and bride's maids
soaked to the skin.

Lenses of cameras wet with unrelenting rain
pounding like waves overhead.
The groom's father came from China
for this wetting.
The bride's father talks of his book
and this infernal rain.
Hors d'oeuvres are served on soggy bread
passed by waiters hopping over puddles
covered by umbrellas
to and from the kitchen
as guests drink and dance and laugh
now undeterred by accents of the storm –

the thundering storm of this wedding
drenched by water falling all around
cold droplets sinking in the ground.

The newly wedded couple
undisturbed by the deluge –
drowned in the torrents
of their never ending love.

Captive

I drew him
deep within –
eyes, mind
skin.

I set my snare cunningly
wooing with words.
I willed him to capture me
envelop me.

We breathed heavily
in the contest
matched perfectly
until our hearts

torn open and exposed
molded into one
and losing sense of time and place
we were home.

The Comfort of Knowing

In early morning
arriving at sleep's destination
I lie quite still
and will you here with me.
For now, you cannot be
but in some spirit way, you are.

I go about the daily needs
of family, work, and home –
with a space inside my mind
behind my smile
in frank and secret wonder
that I am there in yours.

Evenings we recount the day
speak silences between the words
in little conversations
expressing something big, so big –
of some heavenly design
like a hummingbird flirting with the vine.

Our story, yet to be revealed
will unfold
like slowly turning pages in a book.
For now, you are there
and I am here.
Perhaps, it's just the comfort of knowing.

Save Me

Ironing my shirt last night
cigarette drooping from your lips
you pressed my arms against the board
in hot anticipation of the evening.

Shirtless
shoeless
running in the parking lot before breakfast
you flung a towel over a skunk
to free its head from a yogurt cup.

And you wonder why I love you?

You appeared in my life battered, lonely:
Man. Beast.
I heard your wild cry, *Save me, save me!*
branding your mark on my primitive soul.
I answered in the only way I knew –
calling you to me.

Now, I hold you cradling the warmth
strength
savage tenderness –

and I cry to you wildly in the night
calling out,

You save <u>me</u>, save <u>me</u>.

Brevity

Are you happy? I ask him.
He gets up to get some cream for his coffee.
Yes, he says.
When he sits down again
he jabs at his salad.
You know what really makes me happy?
face flushed
voice tight
choking on the words.
It really makes me happy
to be with someone
who wants to know
if I'm happy.

Rosy Room

Blue, dark, dark blue
bedroom walls
mirrored an arctic marriage.
When he left
I needed to rub out the blues.

Choosing three rose hues
in tonal sequence
for walls, ceiling, floor
I savored my choices
as the sun rose rosy in my room.

Then, into the rosy room
arose a man
bearing three pink roses!
With warm arms to hold me
and a passion that was hidden there.

Hidden
under the blue
waiting patiently
to be exposed
in an explosion of rose!

Education in Love

My education in love
a blind man's bluff.
I lurched
with drunken zeal
seeking ardor:

not the kind portrayed in films
products of others' dreams –
but a touch
I could call mine.

At first I found cold lips
arms that would not bend
a wall to lean on
when what I wanted was
a niche.

But when I heard your voice
read the lessons in your eyes
and savored sweetness
like juice from a ripened pear –
I knew.

The night your warm lips
risked their goal
you voyaged to an unknown land.
For me it was that instant
I was welcomed home.

Between Us

What is this force that urges us
toward Nature's pinnacle
then drops us
as we know she would?

Some ancient trick
unbearable test
or that which anchors
something deep and true?

I've fallen into that abyss
where reason takes on wings
and flies away.

Please tether me
firmly on the shore
if you're not holding on
for dear life.

Marry me!

Oh, marry me!
Let us walk upon the dunes.
Marry me. Oh, marry me!
Sing with me some bonny tunes.
Kiss me
and-a-hug me
and roll me in the hay.
Let us swing across the clouds
and come what may!

Newly Wed

Sleeplessness, desire
and chores
of opening the mail
shaving
and stacking dishes
in the sink
blend into one dizzy, giddy blur
as I bump up against you
in the kitchen and bathroom
with delicate restraint
before hot, hungry urges
find us tangling in the sheets.

Fragments

Our life together –
a succession of meals
interrupted by sleep.

I want you to smear your kisses
all over me like jam on bread –
drizzle sweet and thick
sugary words
up and down my spine
to make a signature dessert
you alone can devour.

Celebrating Marriage!

We've just begun
though both of us
have been there twice before.

Spending a quiet night alone
or buying groceries
for our evening meal – a Holiday!

Throwing socks in the dryer
making the bed we've slept in –
what joy!

Reading a book, writing a poem
having dessert
watching a movie on TV

with someone close by
who is loved and loves us.
This is the peace each of us has longed for.

No trip to Europe or nightclub date
could possibly match
this sedentary contentment.

Finally, finally!
Being together
is everything.

Scars

You don't need tattoos
to prove your manliness.
Scars like constellations
zig zag your chest.

Zippered rips
along your hip
and gut
unkindly shut
by careless surgeons –

a shock
when I first saw you
standing nude.

Yet, your graceful acceptance
of these wounds
seared into me a love more deep
than that first kiss that drew me in
and caused me to choose you
my man above all men.

Our flesh blends fiercely
as we trace the patterns
of marks left on us
by others

and dig gently in
to find entrance
through them
to our souls.

Connected at the Hip

No wonder I felt
agitation
restless
on the brink of jumping
out of my skin.

When the orthopedist shook my hand
and said, *All went well* –
mine, shaking in his
firm surgeon's hand
felt as safe as your trust had been
with his precision
working in your bones
repairing, inserting, sewing.

Now I sit
waiting
praying
immobile
while you
anesthetized
dream your dreamless sleep –

I dream awake
your long-held limp
will be erased.

Seventy

At this stage of life
you're supposed to be
winding down
closing up
finishing off
retiring
counting the years left
remembering loves lost
regrets
accomplishments
and small blessings –

that you're sleeping
for the most part
through the night.

That you're able
to hook your bra in the back
button your blouse
bend over to tie your shoes
shampoo your own hair
run out to get the mail
pick the newspaper up
off the driveway.

You can remember birthdays
and lift your grandchildren for a hug.

It's remarkable
to find a new love
at seventy –

someone who adores you
who makes you feel desired
who tenderly holds your face
nibbles your neck
and makes you giggle
like a girl again.

Who would have thought
you'd have such a reason to live
at this stage of life?

Inexpressible

I awake
sleeping next to you
and latch onto your core
like a barnacle on a ship.

You rock me for a while
to satisfy a primal urge
before I reluctantly disengage
returning to my shore.

In the Restaurant

You see the couple
chewing silently
gazing out the window
words only for the waiters.

You pity them
and their boring life –
passion flown
like geese over the pond
as twilight descends upon day.

You have no idea
how they hold each other
when alone –
how her head rests
on his beating heart
his fingers caress
her back and thighs

their murmurs of love
in every embrace
the last thing at night
the first at dawn.

Words they keep
for each other
like expensive chocolates.

LOVE'S DEMISE & OTHER LOSSES

...but love's demise passes
bit by bit –
A clock winding down.
Leaves dropping to the ground.

Love's Mystery

When you're in it
you know what it is.
Your ankles surrender
in the swirling spray
and there's pounding
on the windows of your frame.

You exhale flowers.
Your eyes betray light
at sight of your love's face.
All words are spent
in vain efforts to explain.
It's nameless, shameless.

But when you press
your hand
limbs
against each other's skin –
run your fingers between teeth
across the brow –
whisper secret confidences with
gulps of gasping laughter
you understand the mystery.

You can mark its sudden onset
with a date
or say what it is not
when it's gone
but love's demise passes
bit by bit –
a clock winding down.
Leaves dropping to the ground.

Heart of the matter

Can a broken heart break another heart?
Can two broken hearts
mend each other's?
Can two broken hearts blend into one that is whole?
Can one whole heart break
into two broken ones?

Can your broken heart
reside inside mine
until your heart's content?
Can mine reside in yours?
Would you feel my heart throb,
or skip a beat?

If you love someone with all your heart, and then they break it
do you get back half a heart,
or are you heartless?
Do they give yours back half-heartedly, with a heavy heart
or are they lighthearted?

I'm wearing my heart on my sleeve.
Can we have a heart to heart,
straight from the heart?
I've given you my heart.
It is heart-rending to think of
my heart's desire leaving.

Can one die of a broken heart?
I'd go with you in a heartbeat.
I would follow my heart,
cross my heart,
Sweetheart.

Alone Together

I live alone inside the house
we call our marriage.
You are alone here in the room I sit in, too.
There is a couch we rest on
even though it's empty.
And I'm by myself
when sleeping next to you.

Alone with you I talk
but you don't hear me.
Along with me you walk, but separately.
Once we were so passionately lovers.
Now division is the sum entirety.

How can I be alone *with* you, my darling?
Is there someplace
we can travel on our own?
Could we begin to meet alone together?
And turn this lonely house into a home?

Asylum

I move around inside
your discarded housedress,
dear ancient lady,
reviving its tattered threads
with a strong heart and sinuous limbs.

We are linked now –
I to your ninety-five years
as you attempt to wrench free –
you, to my separation of another sort.

You complain of aches and loneliness
a happier time gone forever.
I have the same.

You fear you are a bother
but you do not bother me
dear, sweet one.
We are sisters.

Some artificial counting of the clock
defines old and young.

Perhaps you notice more
the carrying and chores
I do for you
but I notice
lessons in patience
you teach me.

Love Poem?

This would be a love poem
if pain and disappointment
were erased –
or with gentle tenderness
replaced.
      It's just becoming harder
      to hide embarrassment
      of your ignorance and belligerence.
      I feel disgraced.
Spouting insults at strangers
is justified in your view.
      Spewing smoke into fresh air
      is your "right."
      Or defying requests that are polite.
      They don't apply to you.
I do try
to turn a blind eye, you see.
To make allowances in my mind.
You are not me.
      But there are behaviors
      for grown-ups...
      or at least the one
      with whom I want to be aligned.
(I meet glances of pity
from those who can see
that I suffer indignity.
They understand my anxiety.)
      And the countless times
      I've requested

some moment of affection
    but instead received rejection
makes me think I cannot cling to you
upon reflection.

One Summer's Day

I threw my blanket
boldly on the ground
spread wide
to show its many colors.

Then in some peculiar rage
you whipped it up
and spun it round
mocking its display.

I forgave the rage
with equal rage
that loves
but the blanket is now shut away.

Perhaps one corner at a time
I'll reveal the fine design or
on anniversaries
more –

but I cannot fling it wide
again
to let you
at its core.

Comparisons

I hate
long stories
and cryptic references
in poems

I like
simple
straightforward
revelations

For example:

I had to leave him
and marry someone else
to find out how good
I had it
to begin with

Foreclosure

Our relationship went bankrupt
shortly after the closing
which was a surprise
since you had the exclusive listing
and I thought we had a firm commitment
for joint tenancy after the initial inspection.
Your promissory note
with your credit report
gave you pre-qualification
and there was the sweat equity;
but now we are in debt
because I never knew
you had all those liabilities
when you held an open house in my heart.

I knew the terms of an adjustable loan
could change at any time
and though the amortization schedule
showed much more would be paid
during the life of it
the remaining principal balance outweighs any interest
that was actually accrued.

I didn't know there was depreciation
when the assessment was made
in the final appraisal
and contingencies were placed
in the contract.
So with lack of assets, delinquency
notice of default and partial payment

the maturity has gone
through a modification
and the lack of Truth-in-Lending
has caused the deal to fall apart.

No Longer There

There's a hair's breadth
between happiness and sadness
between the arms enfolding and the cold.
The slightest sigh can signal danger
though the one who sighs be unaware.
The passion of flesh's contact
can fade in morning's sunlit glare
and the love
so ardently offered
is suddenly
no longer there.

Journal Entry

Sunday at dawn
I became aware
you weren't there.
A weight in my heart
plummeted me down the stairs.

You were walking the yard
bright eeriness in your eyes
like fire kindled
after a long period
of gathering wood.

Everything had changed.
You wanted freedom
to be someone
you couldn't be
unless you were apart from me.

I was thinking we were okay
and missed that you'd gone away.
So between the time you said the word
and the time it's come to pass –

There's your empty chest of drawers
your empty vows
my empty bed
and our torn-up photographs.

Last poem to you

Walking together in silence
the final act
in our union of fourteen years
to sign the Divorce Agreement
before a Notary.

We began the drama
on a stage
falling in love
as Edith and Otto Frank.
It was in the silence of our freezes
while Anne was in the spotlight
that we looked into each other's eyes
and found a life together.

So there's a certain irony
that it's in silence
not looking at each other
that we now find a life apart
agreeing
in signing
before an audience of one
to end the play.

Unwelcome Guest

In the half-light of morning
still cousin with my dreams
I rose to meet the sorrow
beckoning to me.

A hollow bead of sadness
arising from my chest
donned its flowing robe
like some unwelcome guest.

It lingered at its washing
and slowly trod the stairs.
It clamored in the kitchen
and kept me from my prayers.

The ghost of a fresh heartache
is visiting with me.
I'm loath to give it hospice
but it will not set me free.

Bedtime Story

It's taken nine months
for my rebirth
from the day you announced,
I want a divorce.

Only now do I find
I gravitate to the center
of our king-size bed
after curled on the right side
where I slept for fourteen years.

It's strange to spread my legs
to own the bed
and know it's mine
as I once did for you
who I thought was mine.

Dirty Linen

Maybe it's time to wash my sheets.
My ex visited in my sleep
three nights now
and it's disturbing;
I liked having him there.
So, it's really time
I pulled them off
and stuffed them in the washer
along with my other soiled dreams.

Failed Marriages?

Two failed marriages –
first Mom's
then mine.
Her first of twenty-three years
bore three children.
My first of twenty-three years
bore three children.
Her second saw fifteen anniversaries
before he left her for his secretary.
My second saw fourteen
before he left me for another actress.
Can you call it a failed marriage
when children have been brought forth
or when you share a bed, a house
with the same spouse
for eight thousand three hundred ninety-five
nights and days –
or even
four thousand seven hundred forty-five
more or less?
If you had died during one of those spans –
would it be called successful?

Half-Life

Her clothes hang in half a closet.
Her head rests in half a bed.
Half-a-mind-to-matter suits her.
She'll lead a half-life
when he's dead.

Grieving

layering
her mourning clothing
layer upon layer of clothing

still
she cannot still the moaning
stifle the awful moaning
seeping from the hollow
the unfathomable hollow

raising
arms crossing her brow
she raises up her clothing
pulling at her elbows
as at weeds
pulling at her widow's weeds

digging
cutting with her nails
digging with her nails
earthy arms
cutting at the root of her
earth-warm, empty arms

wailing
weeping with the moaning
seeping from the hollow

weeping
wailing at the mention
moaning at the mem'ry

Grieving

Apron #1

Red and white checks
tied at the waist:
a small apron,
not much for covering.
Just enough to say,
I'm a wife.
I cook pot roasts and potatoes.
I set the table with clean linen napkins
and never skip dessert.
(My husband expects it.
He's French, you know.)

Years from now he'll leave me
for that lazy cow
who doesn't cook or clean
or do much more
than help him with his crosswords
and, I suppose, she's good in bed.
He had cross words for me, too,
but not the kind I dared to finish
as I'd scrape his plates and slip them
into hot, soapy water.

Apron #2

Red and white checks
around Mommy's waist
so pretty in a big bow.
Or I see it hanging
blowing to and fro
the clothespins bouncing up and down
and know
there'll be something good for dinner
and cake for dessert
and sweet-smelling napkins
fresh off the line
and a steam-pressed tablecloth.
But, no matter what,
Daddy yells
and Mommy tells me,
No, Honey, it's all right.
I don't need help with the dishes.
You can go and play.

Lost in New Jersey

August, 1955
Newark, NJ

Mom sent me with my father
in the hot DeSoto –
its leather seats scorching
my nine-year-old legs.
Dad stubbed out his cigarette
put on his realty agent's smile
and entered the divorcee's
one-bedroom bungalow.
I sat there for *forever*
as I saw the shades pulled down.
He said I couldn't go with him.
He told my mom
he'd been making a big sale.

March, 1982
Norwalk, CT

Our white Mercedes
with no heat
was useless in New England
when we moved up north from Florida.
We hoped to rent a house
with no job, no address
no relations there.
But the landlord in Norwalk
eyed the '68 Mercedes
and gave us keys

to his duplex –
for me, my husband, and three kids –
no questions asked.

I wondered how the trust
my mother lost
in Newark
August, 1955 –
was found
in Norwalk
by this man –
March, 1982.

Red

Almost pageantry, that
red.

Burning sunset sails
red.

Mother's lipstick
red.

Scarlet letter
red.

Matador's muleta
red.

Iron in the fire
red.

Seething bull
red.

Broken hymen seeping
on my bed

red.

Gone

You've gone white
racing down the beach
to find our daughter.
It is in this flash
sharper than any other
your father-love burns.
And Hell would do well
to throw her out
before you'd find her there.

Fourteen

Gorgeous boy striding
legs flailing side to side
as you chase the fleeting ball.
You have not learned to run them straight yet
and they get away from you.
Forcing gulped air down a slender neck
I hear your voice squeak, squeaking.
Embarrassed
your eyes seek mine across the field.
I have caught your glance and understand.
My boy is brinking
to a man.

In the dark bathroom
we meet each other's startled eyes
at midnight.
I have heard your bed squeak, squeaking
and have come to see
if you are well.
Embarrassed
you smile as you wash your hands.
I have caught a glimpse of your nude skin
and understand.

My boy is leaving.
He has gone – legs flailing.
He has not learned to run them straight yet
and they get away from him.
My boy is brinking
to a man.

Delivery

The mother
paralyzed with fear
heart racing
panting brief bursts of prayer
as camera hums
and details are recorded
to report to those
who hunger for the news.

The son
ripped from the world he has known
to a future of uncertainty.
There is no turning back.
A sentence is delivered.

Escorted down the passageway
he cries,
facing Life.

little marriages

on the platform
passengers-in-waiting
jockey for a door
bodies pressed
as train pulls in
a conjugal metaphor

consultation with the sky
eyes upon the clock
coffee held in practiced art
sipped cautiously while hot

extending nonchalant embrace
a dull expression on his face
the businessman with news spread wide
stakes his claim for space

with travelers pairing off
to go to work and back again
brushing shoulders
jostling hips
rubbing knees in perfect time

clacking cars on tracks
candid conversation
the daily ride
sometimes interrupted
by a suicide.

Begging Pardon of a Squirrel

Please forgive me
dear unnamed, untamed
suicidal creature
that ran under my tires
before I had a chance
to veer away.

What could I do?
For a second
I thought of stopping
to help you escape
your horror.

But I squashed the idea
for fear of being nauseated
more than of appearing
foolish, as other cars zoomed
across your soon to be dead little body.

But I'm thinking of you still –
long after this morning's squirrel-slaughter –
so sad for having ended your life's brief journey
perhaps on a mission to feed babies
or just playing "dare" with friends.

Therefore, I'm penning these few lines
my small, deceased
co-inhabitant of our earth;
and though you've preceded me
I'll join you someday –
just hopefully not in the same way.

Breasts

We bone them, pound and stuff them
and proudly pass them to our guests
we share them

We're fond of them when they are cooked
or placed into our mouths and shook
we want them

We tug them with our baby lips
and with our full-grown fingertips
we touch them

We squeeze them with our tiny hands
and suck the milk from swollen glands
we pat them

We put them into wired cups
we tighten them and press them up
we bind them

We measure size to hold them in
or swing them freely in the wind
we flaunt them

We want them larger than they are
or not so cumbersome by far
we fix them

We search for lumps or hidden mass
we crush them between plates of glass
we probe them

We ogle, use, they sag, they bruise
and if the diagnosis proves
we lose them

But when in poetry or art
breasts inspire the artist's heart
and all the bliss that comes from this
we praise them

Crazy Horse

The fire warms the earth.
Drums stir my blood
into red hot frenzy.
My heart begins to race.

There are dances to be danced
war-paint to be drawn upon our faces
scores to settle
scorched lands to be reclaimed.

This tomahawk sings
as it rises then falls
and rests in my palm
ready for the strike –

its sharp edge
my sharp eyes
these sharp teeth
meld and our whole being

swells with desire
to appease our Mother Earth
seek calm in between stormy clouds
dry tears our people have wept

in mourning for
what was ours –
what has gone forever.
I rail and rail

and rail.

A Split Second

There's a split second
between a misstep
and the moment you land
splat! on your face
when you know
you have lost control.

You scream, *NO!*
but it doesn't change a thing.
As you fly forward
you see your future clearly.
Everything you planned
for this day and coming months
is gone.

You wish the clock
could turn back
just an instant
where you would look
more carefully
and cheerfully continue
on your way.

But you cannot turn it back.
You cry out in pain and shame.
You appear to be
just some old woman who falls –
who cannot move forward
or stand up
because her bones
have shattered to pieces
in an instant.

Shock, trauma, regrets
shame, pain
converge in a split second
that will grow longer and linger
and seat itself
in your memory and your body.

A scene to play
over and over and over.

In the Middle of it All

1.

There's a good-sized chunk
of chocolate cake
left-over from my party.

2.

I bought stamps at the post office
and mailed some Christmas cards.
I still have a few to write.

3.

Laundry is in the dryer.
waiting to be folded
and brought upstairs.

4.

I'm hoping to hear
that my play is accepted
for the Spring Poetry Festival.

5.

I'm working on a new poem.

6.

Half a chicken is in the fridge
and the hard-boiled eggs
are ready to be devilled.

7.

All the presents
I've purchased
need to be wrapped.

8.
My son's family might come
New Year's weekend.
He'll let me know.

9.
I washed the dishes
and stacked them
on the side, to dry.

10.
My daughter texted
that she'll call me
tomorrow.

11.
The coffee pot
is set-up
ready for morning.

12.
There's a check I'm expecting
for my care of a woman
with dementia.

13.
I began reading
an interesting book:
Earth Abides.

14.
I put on my nightgown
brushed my teeth
and climbed into bed.

15.

And for no clear reason why,
in the middle of it all
I died.

MEMORIES

pressing into my memory
the warm laundry fragrance
rising into the atmosphere

Ironing

Sharing a cold cola
with my mother
I'd talk about school
and watch her
sprinkle the clothes
roll them in a tight loaf
let them rest
spread them across the board
hear the sputter and hiss
as she'd steam
all the wrinkles
side to side
top to bottom
kneading them
pressing into my memory
the warm laundry fragrance
rising into the atmosphere
press
press
pressing
with laughter and confidences.
Shaping the bread of my life.

The Lesson

Skipping gaily along
to first day
of fourth grade
in Jefferson School –
my brand-new school
in our New Jersey neighborhood –
the boys made quacking sounds
across the street
as they raggedly stomped
and rough-housed
on their way in the same direction
sneering, pointing, and whooping
at my "big feet."
I was eight years old, thin, and short.
My shiny patent-leather size six shoes
gleamed in the sunlight.
I did look like a duck!

But I marched bravely on
responding to their jeers
by keeping my mouth sealed tight
body stiff,
chin held high but quavering.

At home I cried angry tears
while mother gave me comfort
and a lesson I'd not forget.
She'd read it somewhere –
I wept because I had no shoes
until I saw a man who had no feet.

And though my feet
grew to be size ten
before they stopped –
I have been grateful
that I have them
ever since.

Young Girls in White Blouses

nubs not yet blown
clump in the playground
to whisper dark secrets

about boys they'll kiss
after hating them first –
this is the way they learn
tension and longing.

Dreaming in sweet sheets
they clutch at their pillows
and fantasize boy-men
who'll come when they've grown.

They'll learn mothers' mysteries
who just smile wistfully
when asked by their daughters
where fathers have gone.

But mothers don't answer
or teachers won't tell
so playground lore ends
with a ring of the bell.

Au Revoir Paris; 1969

On my ill-fated
date with escargot
in a French restaurant
après le diner

I stared at the stained *tapissiere*
in my Parisian hotel room
for three days
on my first trip to France.

I could not rise from my bed
despite cajoling of my friend's Père
eager to move on to Spain.
He hated to wait

for me to be strong
to be weakly led
to the rented Citroen
he drove at breakneck speed

along treacherous roads
across the Pyrenees.
I nearly fainted with fear
lying in the back seat

eyes squeezed tight.
So much for the grand tour.
But Spain was good
for my constitution.

I recovered to savor
fascinating Spanish *platos*
of fish and rice
and sweet sangria.

The promised trip to Pamplona
for the running of the bulls
was stamped out
as too perilous.

So, it was off to San Sebastian
and its famous film festival.
But my friend's father
tried to tear me away

from this promising picturesque
seaport town and its cinema
racing through Europe as he was
but I refused

wanting to bask in the Basque.

I met a handsome Swede
for a three-day romance.
He escorted me to my train
for Madrid

and stood too long in the aisle
kissing me goodbye.
As the train began to roll
he jumped off

tearing his favorite blue sweater
he later wrote in a letter.
But *it was worth it*
he told concerned bystanders.

She was a beautiful American girl.

The Suitcase

She went off to college
with her bright white
American Tourister –
a good brand that would last.
Her mom saved all her pennies
to purchase it with its
pockets that snapped in with
blue satin lining and ties.
After graduation
she took it to Luxembourg
on the plane
anticipating a European tour by car
with her girlfriend
and her girlfriend's father –
but something went awry
and she found herself
on a train to Madrid alone
and then hitchhiking
with her American boyfriend –
the white American Tourister
suitcase ever by her side.
When she returned home from Europe
by ship
the American Tourister
sailed along, as well.
It also made the trips
to Boston and New York, to
Connecticut, Massachusetts, Maryland, Bahamas,
Florida, California, Cape Cod,
and everywhere she went
for forty years.

It never got lost, never let her down.
Now it sits in her basement,
slightly mildewed
filled with certificates, old documents
and maps.

Just one more trip, it silently pleads,
begging to be used appropriately.

But she's moved on to
wheeled carry-ons and backpacks
and only opens that now
ivory-colored case
when she's searching for those
old memories.

Harlem Prep School, 1969

You take your names from Africa
to replace your given ones
like Maitefa Angaza, Hailu
and Melvin's now "Black Power" –
creating new identities
prompting me to question mine.

Fragrant ethnic spices permeate your skin.
Your school attire – beads, and woven cloths
wrapped 'round your Afros and your limbs –
reveal your artistry.

Bracelets chime as you walk and dance
to drumbeat sounds
throughout this former grocery store –
a brand-new concept: open classrooms.
The noisy lectures echo all around
while you debate your views
competing to be heard
with Harlem's traffic noise that plays
a steady beat from the street
adding its vibrations
to the music of this special space.

You were selected high school dropouts
to be prepped for college.
I was privileged to be hired here
to learn with you
of Langston, James, Amiri, Stokely
and to share your admiration

of Nina, Herbie, Miles –
all and more who enter
your enthusiastic conversations.

Some students need escape
from roaches, rats, and poverty
stabbings, crack dens, tenements of perverts
whores and drunks –

and some are here to change conditions
with what an education brings.

Ritual

I have sneaked cigarettes one by one
on the back porch in the moon's gaze
for so many years
it's atonement for my tears.

In my old, long dresses
loose around the knees
hair struggling to be free
from the knot at the back;
bare feet in the summer
or slippers when it's frosty cold –

this gnawing
half between my throat's cry
and the button pressing on my skin
sets me to thinking of the need.

I clatter dishes, pots, and pans
so no one dares approach
nor notices when it's gone.
It's just relief.

I confess my reasons to the moon
which answers in a cricket's tune.
It knows full well my hurting soul
and winks its pardon
with a pale eye.

Second Chance

I
Remember as a child
sitting in the back seat
of your father's Chevrolet
as he drove along country roads
in autumn?
And you could imagine yourself
carelessly running through the woods
stirring up the leaves
wanting to have nature all over you
wrap its arms around you
and let you nuzzle its soft mossy earth?

II
Or passing a grassy hill
in your adolescence
as your parents argued in the front seat
you'd spy a little town in the distance
the church steeple
peeking up over the hilltop
and you wanted to jump out of the car
run onto the green field
tumble through the overgrowth
and knock on the door of the sexton
who was just sitting down to dinner.
You'd say you were an orphan
who had run away
and needed a place to hide
and you were hungry
and could he spare a little soup
and a mat near the fire for the night?

III

Or you were a young mother
sitting up front in the passenger seat
turning to look at the father of your children
and then back at the sleeping children
and wonder where you would be now
if you had run away
with the traveling poet
who sang to you one night
after your first baby was born –
played his guitar for you
and made you feel beautiful and desired
and could see into your soul?

IV

And as you recall those lost longings
lying in your bed one September morning
remembering what you didn't do
because you were responsible
or obedient, or dependable
or too old for fantasies –
something stirs within you.
This something tells you
to go down to the great, rich sea
outside your doorway
with its crashing waves
and deep, uncertain waters
before it is too late.

V

And so you step out of the comfort
of your land-locked room

and go to the shore where riotous waves
beckon you to slip underneath
and let it swallow you up –
toss you playfully about
and wash over your body –
reach up under your bed clothes
to cleanse your cold skin
and tease the young woman out of you
until you are floating and arching
and sweetly aching
swimming and gliding
and giddy with gratitude
that you haven't missed your chance.

Carry Me Back

The fragrance of sweet-scented cigars
lifts me in the rickety elevator
to my first job on the 17th floor
at a Philadelphia insurance company
hired by two old men
who puffed inexorable smoke
into the building's walls.

A spray of White Shoulders
and that slutty senior high school girl appears
who drenched daily in the pungent stuff
sending a message to all
that she is in the halls.

A sniff of Jean Nate and I'm at college
my sorority sisters bathing in it
as we powdered and splashed.
A whiff of scotch
and I'm doubled over the toilet bowl
in my boyfriend's upper crust apartment.

Essence of rose petals flies me over
oceans, cities, plains to Israel
on pilgrimage to holy places
and bougainvillea sends me
straight down to Bahamas
where we lived three months
awaiting work visas to teach.

My mother is Emeraude
the Oriental perfume

permeating her trousseau
of silks and satins
that became my dress-up clothes
when I acted out movie stars, nuns
cowgirls and queens.

Give me the scent of tobacco
in the pocket of a shirt
and I'm back on my father's lap
cradled in his arms as I cried
for whatever reasons little girls cry

his Pall Malls the aroma
of a loving Dad
forever.

Old Friends
(for Nina)

Our History sat at lunch with us
delighting in our friendship
enjoying the warmth of our laughter
not saying a word.

It would have monopolized
the conversation
if it interrupted
while we were catching up.

We made the same menu selections:
an Arnold Palmer, seafood chowder,
ginger shrimp salad,
warm bread and butter.

We asked the waiter,
learning the delicious butter
was Grassland,
made since 1911.

We touched on old subjects
and new ones.
There's never enough time
for all we'd like to share.

After we paid the bill
we hugged and said,
I love you,
and went our separate ways.

Our History hung behind
in the parking lot
taking down all the details
to add to our story.

Smiling
as we drove away.

Remembrance

In the windows of my memory
flowers line the paths
or grow in fenced-in patches.

Where there were weeds fighting to survive
a tug from the earth
created garden's splendor.

Each pane of glass holds
a child's birth and passing years.
Laughter, cries, anger.
Three children
playing, growing, loving.
Waving their goodbyes.

Three other frames
hold memories with husbands
sharply etched into my mind
or vaguely stored there.
Affection for all three in varying degrees.

Mother and Father suddenly appear
but glaring sun fades those years
where I as child and woman intertwine.

So many dwellings comprise my life.
Dreams tangle memories
into many rooms revisited in sleep.

Moving in, moving out of homes
climbing stairs

exploring all the floors and doors
crevices, and plot lines.

I reminisce repeatedly in my sleep
forced to reconcile mistakes
forsaken longings.

Exposed

A catch of breath
came over me
watching the documentary.
Nothing that was said
not a memory –
but transported
for an instant
to the 1960's –
just long enough to recall
feelings
once strongly felt
by a younger me.

Part of myself was there
where what would become of me
was still an unknown mystery
and the poignancy
of seeing now
my unremarkable history.

Recycled

Never enough
for something extra.
When the ice cream truck
came jingling
down our street

Mom would yell for me
to come in
and have some soup
or read a book
'til he was gone.

A nickel for a popsicle
much too dear.
A quarter for dues
in my Brownie troop
put my father in a rage.

With Mother's thrift
came creativity –
do over, remake
transform hand-me-downs
from my cousins

into stylish
new dresses and hats.
Her motto:
Waste not, want not.
I also cling to that.

My husband finds questionable
left-overs in the fridge
but has learned to ask before tossing –
I've cautioned him
it may still have some use.

I do not hoard
but I do hesitate
before disposal.
Could it have another life?
I certainly have.

Discarded by my former spouse
I'm now transformed
remade
recycled –
new and extra special.

Reels

After dinner and dessert
we settled down to watch home movies
transferred for preservation
from reels to DVDs.

I relived my early years of marriage
and first child, a happy boy
forever rolling down the dunes.

Grandparents appeared glancing with smiles
at the camera, but it too soon turned
onto vistas of waves, or trees and sky.

My mother with child walking –
but she'd flit just ahead or to the side
or retreat behind the lens.

I willed the camera
to hold on her face
to grasp her thoughts from back then
or frame a close-up of
her young smooth skin.

Too quickly it passed over
to capture, instead, a mountain
that will ever be there –
or parades with strangers in forgotten towns.

But the faces
of family and friends
so many now gone.

My breath caught and choked.
Tears spilled as ones once loved
slipped past.

And that night my sons laughed with me –
hard –
watching home movies
of fleeting years and lives gone by.

SENSE OF PLACE

Carnival
In our rooms we see it from a distance
Creeping through our windows in the night
Swelling all our thoughts with its insistence
Filling up our senses with the light.

The hurly-burly music starts its calling
The carnie people generate a whine
The barkers cry of lady luck's persistence
And suddenly we find ourselves in line.

Jersey Girl

Guys with their slick D.A.'s
took me for a ride
in their souped up Chevrolets
trailing cigarette smoke out the sides
of their mouths, so cool
to this sophomore
straight from Catholic school.
Blowing smoke rings to impress
me in my home-made cotton sundress,
speeding down the main drag
driving with their knees
prompting prayers under my breath,
a hundred
Dear Jeez-us, please protect me's!

And the petting I denied
though they tried and tried
(I'd always get my monthly "friend"
early inexplicably.
Was it God's way of protecting
me and my virginity?)

On the strip, on summer holiday
between the ocean and the bay
I yearned for something more
in my teen years down the shore.
Though I didn't know just what it was
or what I hungered for
in my naïve virgin's sixteen-year-old skin
somehow, I knew it was a sin.

Dibble's Exhibition

Sunday at four
it's misting out
and chill for June.
A step inside
and there we are
inside Dibble's head.

What can be said
now that the pith is up
and hanging on the wall?
I want to screech
I know you now
(or think I do)
or *Thank you for sharing*
so much with me!
But I only say
I love your stuff.
It was pleasant,
and
Goodbye.

Diner Dance

Stoop and sway –
two cups of coffee on the way.
Sashay to the right.
Looks like a long and busy night.
Slide to the left
three more swoop in.
Ring up the bill
I'm staying trim!
A cheerful smile
Watch out! It's hot!
A graceful turn
with coffee pot.
French fries, a burger
on the double!
(That customer always
gives me trouble!)

Sugar House

Steaming sugar
in rows of pails
sapped along the maple roads
from cold Vermont hills.

Mountain men stroke their beards
in sweet, heated air
inside a rough-hewn house
and stoke the wood to boil the water
to heat the sap to make the syrup.

Reticent men slowly open up the tale
as they see I am intrigued –
tap a cup and pass it round.
Liquid sugar floating on a warm cloud.

The Gift

I like the snowstorm
that gathers its force at night
and when I turn on my porch light
I see the huge flakes rushing down the street
like a gang taking over the neighborhood.
I know it won't be safe to go out
until the all-clear sounds
the day after tomorrow.

The morning radio announces
everyone should stay at home
so I, cheerfully compliant
curl up in pajamas all day long
enjoying the white drifts and swags
like bleached laundry hanging on a line.
Oh, yes, I'll join the others in a uniform
of down jacket, cap, and gloves
armed with shovel to displace the havoc wreaked upon us.

But for now this change in tempo
to enforced seclusion, cup of cocoa
and contemplation
is more welcome than a planned vacation –
as it arrived effortlessly
presenting me
the unexpected gift of time.

Winter's Melody

I walked into the woods behind my house
to find the trees holding a formal
in their cotillion finery –
some branches bowing low
frozen heavy with organza,
others stiff with tulle
as they curtsied
in their white ball gowns
to the taller trees
standing proudly in a row,
boughs spread as though
asking to have this dance
nodding slightly to the wind's refrain.

A neighbor played his shovel like a drum –
a scrape, a brush
or muffled in a tom-tom beat
rhythmically swishing back and forth
across his driveway.

The sun beamed its rays
through the waving limbs
over the ballroom floor
inviting me to join the dancing shadows,
and unable to resist,
I stepped into their circle.

Cape Cod Life

Cape Codders
who live by the sea
and look at stars

breathing salt air
painting pretty scenes
of wind-blown hair

aren't the Cape Codders
who sleep in cars
and never see the sea

for necessity
of keeping themselves fed
or finding their child a bed

and not enough time in the day
to while away
and sing of its charms

as they seek any jobs
to buy clothes and fuel
to keep warm.

Interview with Mrs. Frank Blank

Well, I never thought much about it before...
I guess there's not much to say.
I mean, my mind's a blank, hee hee.
But when I'm asked to fill in the blanks
I take it very personally.
I think it's nice you want to know about me.
I'm Blanche Blank, from Blaine, Maine.
In 2008, I voted for McCain.

My husband, Frank, works
at Carte Blanche Bank.
My daughter, Bianca, sews blankets,
and my son, Frank, Jr.
manages Plate Glass Unlimited.

There's been no effect on us whatsoever
having to live with a blank identity.
We're just like everyone else.
I guess you'd say, we're an average family
with no unusual tendencies;
no claims to fame.
We mind our own business
and hope others do the same.
We like our potatoes white –
our food unseasoned –
our fences well-made.
Charity begins at home, we always say.
Birds of a feather flock together.
Live and let live.
They won't catch us stepping out of line.

We keep our noses clean
if you know what I mean.
We don't go in for any of that
artsy nonsense
if you'll pardon the expression.
We're just plain folks, to put it bluntly.
We don't dispute authority.
We're just your normal moral majority.

At the Perfumer's

Could the palette include essential oils
with rich woody notes
mixed with amber for warmth
and fragrance of spice?

I don't want a scent that fades.
I want an expression of earthiness
with a signature that trails its aroma
long after I've left the room.

And be certain to infuse natural extracts
of authenticity –
absolute sincerity, trust, perseverance
and a hefty splash of rebellion.
These must be layered in accordance
with one another.

A bouquet of floral overtones won't do.
I'm a wildflower, not a shrinking violet.
Above all, create a pure blend
that permeates inspiration.

Oh! I almost forgot!
Is there something in your formulary
you can insert for boundless energy?
I'm planning to wear it every day.

Please pour it in a refillable bottle
with a mesh atomizer
so I can mist it
wherever I go.

The flacon needs to be sturdy
but appealing to the eye.
It will be displayed –
not hidden away
behind cabinet doors.

Finally,
I'd like it delivered
in a box
wrapped in a silver lining.

Did you get all that?
As she turned to leave
he called out to her.
She turned back,
thought for a moment
and with a confident smile, replied

The label?
Oh,
it should say:
C'est moi.

Homeland

I am French.
In winter
when the snow clings thickly to the wall
I sit at my table by the window
drinking café noir
and smoking Gauloises.

By spring I am metamorphosing
into my summer Spaniard
who pulls her hair back tightly
neatly in a bun
wears flashing earrings, swirling skirts
and leather sandals.

With autumn, I move North again
across the Pyrenees up to England
drawing my petticoats in
freeing my hair to the wind
and walking briskly
anxiously
toward my winter state.

Traveler's Tale

What is the story behind that dress?
He asks the fortune teller.

She answers with a well-worn tale.
I bought it at a thrift shop.

But in the shadow of the candlelight
she reminisces
how she stole the favorite gown
of the bijou woman
from a caravan in Jacca
and wrapped her lover's flag
around her waist
as she danced beneath the stars.

Hostage

My flamenco dancer
seized me
as I leapt late
out of bed
dashed to dress
and raced for the train.
No time for thought
I donned the long red skirt
black silk shirt
bracelets and silver-hoop earrings.
I plastered red lipstick
and black charcoal eyes
onto my face
and shook my shoulders
as I jigged and jangled
down the hall
to my office.

Tuesday in July

The wind is hot and iris-scented
with promises of storm ahead.
The sky is slate outside her window
reminders of the things he's said.

Her smile is full of summer senses
of barefoot walks on water's edge.
She shares a glance with knowing silence:
the rain will wash the privet hedge.

Tree and Moon Embrace

Weary of the moon's rebuff
on his journey past each night
never pausing to rest
on her limbs
despite extending them
in longing –

she perceived
on this cloudy night
his wanton visage
as an invitation
and in supplication
drew him into her.

He lingered for a moment
touched by her need.
Her soothing strokes
stirred his desire
to return each time his phase was low
and full of yearning.

No Explanation Necessary

We now live in a world:
where an Asian mom shops with
her African American children
and no one does a double take.

Where all over our TVs
interracial couples play games
with their multi-toned kids
in beautiful suburban neighborhoods –
their white friends joining in.

We see two dads carrying baby twins
in their tattooed arms
walking on the streets of P'town
and we barely break our stride.

We see what looks like a little girl's grandpa
and learn he is her dad.
And some grandparents are raising
their children's children.

Teachers have classes of students
with names they've never seen
but learn to pronounce:
Xiomara, Qitura, Shoghi.

Women are seen wearing veils
in the street or offices
as a sign of reverence –
not the latest fashion.

We push 1 on a call
to hear the message in English.
Bathroom signs indicate
"self-identified" women or men.

We're learning to refer
to what used to be a him or her
as "they." It's change.

We can embrace it and rejoice
or reject it and despair.
It's here.
No explanation necessary.

Tilling Winter's Soil

I'm digging up old poetry
unearthing inspiration
when you tap at the window
motioning urgently
mouthing something
I can't hear
the music is too loud

so we make funny faces until
your insistence
forces me to come outside.
Did you ever see baby earthworms?
Is that what's so important?
But you are lifting a stone, and I laugh
as I witness the miracle.

Encounter

The man reading his paper
at the coffee shop
got up and left
when I sat down.

The folding of his paper
and the leaving
seemed eerily familiar.

Such a brief moment was shared
in the same space
where our lives intersected
then moved apart.

SPIRITUAL CONTEMPLATIONS

Guardedly
our hopes have opened
choking back alarm
until we cautiously approach
to reconcile with our sisters
and our brothers.

Human Race Reunited

Kindred of different shades
birthed in the same soil
but ripped apart with lightning flash
and flung asunder
from our Mother.

We settled
where we grew
learned trades, farmed acres
raised families and villages
forgetting what was missing.

But, a stirring
in the patterns
like sand blown off by monks
shifted at our centers
and whispered what we'd lost.

Warily
we inched through mud
trod roads strewn with ruts
lumbered through the thicket
searching for each other.

Guardedly our hopes have opened
choking back alarm
until we cautiously approach
to reconcile with our sisters
and our brothers.

In unison
hands will till the rows
with rhythmic motions
smooth away the stones
until the earth sings.

The ache of barren land
singed and burned beneath the sun
will be replaced by new growth
in joyful recognition of reconciliation
with the reaping of the grain.

Confession

Bless me Father for I have sinned
the confession begins.
The confessional is narrow
with a hard bench where you kneel.
The priest slides the screen door open
with a bang.

Now you are to whisper in his ear
childish sins you've committed.
It's rehearsal for the times
later on in life
when real sins
have come to pay their dues.

Desolee

Such a lovely way
to say, *I'm sorry.*

It's softer than, *Sorry!*
that forcefully spits
with hissing sibilance.

But with *desolee*
I am desolate, disconsolate.
I live in a wasteland of error.

And in that confession
I humbly request
the one I have transgressed

bestow the blessed grace
of absolution.

When Spirits Meet and Bond

as hands touch with *Hello*
others cannot understand
this instant recognition
of the light inside another
and it cannot be explained.

It's love of a different nature
that rises into life
when two
like souls
collide.

When that mystical spirit
leaps out of the stranger
discovering its kindred
as if finding one who has been lost
after lifetimes of search –

a magnetic field surrounds them
and others back away.
The force so powerful –
a mystery.
The face of joy.

Going Home

Driving east on sixty-six
skies are darkening

Steady humming of the wheels
whistles to the promise of the road

Golden arrows of the sun
work the words into my song

I'm going home

Radio sends *Amazing Grace*
peaceful message from above

The weary place that holds my heart
is bringing love

No fiery bombs around my head
explosions' sound on distant lands

An empty cot that was my bed
the gun gone from my hands

God's here in every tree I pass
the strip malls and the blades of grass

He was there too in boarded homes
with metal shards and broken glass

How many houses in this world
could be the one where I turn in

But on I drive with gift of life
for family, the kids, my wife

And finally to the doorstep
of the place I live

Faith in Surgical Day Care

It's 6 a.m. and the first arrivals
for scheduled surgery
line up at my station.

They're tired and hungry
hurting and vulnerable,
scared.

I've seen
all types of humanity
pass through those doors.

Young mothers with babies,
tough guys,
the deaf and the blind,
middle-aged husbands
and wives.

The elderly
with a spouse, if they're lucky
a compassionate friend,
or sometimes alone.

In wheelchairs or crutches,
or walkers,
or handcuffs.

All races, religions, and cultures.
Americans, Germans, Brazilians, Chinese.
World citizens.

They are united
in a common faith:
the doctor will heal them
and they will be made well.

Mariupol Hotel

Checkerboard tiles pulse with blood.
Walls, windows, roofs caved in
atop the bodies piled there
under smoke and flaming skies.

No peaceful respite for the guests.
No three-tiered wedding cake
lovingly baked by the bride's Baba.
No groom or bride or priest.
No musicians playing
for the joyful dancing.

Doves sweep them gently
one by one
into caskets made of earth
for their final resting place,
each plot inscribed by wings,
not with Aleksander, Anastasia
Tato, Mama, Tio, Tia, but
human, human, human, human.

My tears can't heal your pain

They cannot remove
the chain around your wrists
the target on your back
the knee on your neck
the pleas that seep out of you
      in labored breaths
           then choking gasps
                until the final sigh.

I want to stand with you
in suffering
in celebration
challenge eyes that are blind
      to your blessed creation
the beauty of your skin
      in its varied hues of earth
the powers of your mind
      that have long endured subjugation
your strong spirit
      that's withstood oppression
through centuries of hardship.

This I want to do
to prove my love
as I expose my heart for you.

Because
      my tears
           can't heal
                your pain.

Again

My approach to writing this poem
has been altered
by LeRoi (now Amiri) Jones (now Baraka)
much as my life was altered in the sixties
when his words inflamed the fire in my heart
and led me to Harlem Prep
to strive to make amends for my "whitehood"
and "save" the black youth
who taught me.

My eyes are opened again
again to the ever-present
pain, injustice, irony,
"white-teeth-hiding false-words"
experience of my
darker-skins family.

What can be the salve
the balm
for villainy
crime?

Can we form a circle
take hands
shout our anger
share our tears
and heal wounds of Racism
screaming so many years
through our veins

contaminating our water
our earth?

Not close our eyes
again?

Hoeing

Uniting centuries of women and men
a symphony of musicians
a chorus of carolers
performing this movement

engaged in a relationship
to disentangle roots
disturb unseeded soil
untie knots of inactivity
dig up fallow, dense earth

till the clay
rid the weeds
rake, smooth
cultivate
take control

make sense
out of days
of disorder
find peace

work
one row at a time
many times in a row
reach, stretch
pull back

a meditation
a prayer
a plan
a hope
growth

Falling Angels

Who was first
to jump
that fateful day
to face a horror
of sure death
by crushing blow
avoiding
sure death
by smoke and fire?

During
the long
hideous
descent
first
right side up
then
upside-down
what were
the final
thoughts?

In the moments
of free-fall
was there
recounting
of one's deeds
or was there
regret
and a wish

to return
to the ledge
of the burning
inferno?

Did the couple
holding hands
express vows
of undying love?

Did the mother
call out
to her children
the son
cry for his mother,
the business
men and women
beg pardon
for time
not spent
with families?

Was there prayer?

Did God
cradle
the falling man
whisper
in his ear
reassuring
he would be safe?

Was there fear

time for tears

or before

the very

end

was

there

only

peace?

Oncology Nursery Rhyme

I see them walking to and fro
through my window
I see them go

Some are fat and some are thin
I see them walking
as they go in
I see them walking
out again

Not much laughter
Somewhat grim

Somewhat paler as the days go by
Somewhat balder and less spry
Always hopeful, some do cry
In every weather, wet or dry

It may have settled in her breast
Or in his liver or in his chest
Or in her brain or on her skin
I see them walking as they go in
I see them walking out again

And when the therapy is finished
And that devil disease has been diminished
I hope to God they're free at last
And I won't have to see them pass

Anymore to and fro
Through my sparkling window glass.

On My Birthday

A long-time friend
died on my birthday.
I was partying with gifts, tributes, and cake,
as he drew his final breath.
While my family gathered 'round
to sing and celebrate,
his assembled by his side to bid farewell.

When last we met, we hugged and said,
It's good to see you!
I thought I'd run into him again.
I guess our friendship is the glue
that will remain.
Our mortal bodies cannot last.
I only hope there truly is an after-life
and he'll be there to greet me with
It's good to see you!
whenever I arrive.

Time

How much time do you have left?
Can it be measured in
teaspoons
minutes
days
years?

What would you do if you knew
tomorrow was your last?
Should it be any different than
if you didn't know?

Because it always could be
and one day it will be.

So, what will you do now –
right now, this minute?
It's all we really know.

We could walk out that door
thinking we're going to the store,
and BANG! The end.
Even sitting right here
we could be talking and suddenly...

So be grateful.
Grateful for each moment.
Be thankful for those in your life
who have given to you or taken away.

It's all been a journey to today
and you are here through twists and turns
of each minute, each day, each year
and each teaspoon.

Hopefully, the teaspoon
was sometimes dipped in honey.

When I Am Dead

gather not
to gaze upon the empty shell
that was a woman.
Not to weep for the soul
that is happy with God.

Rather
band together and clasp hands.
Gaze upon the clear and fading eyes,
the white and rotting teeth,
the full and sunken cheeks.

Stroke one another's hair
and laugh and sing together
and love them all,
if you loved me.

Resurrection

I thought
it had been locked up
with its pain
and the gatekeeper gone
to destination unknown
on the train –

or the gravedigger with his spade
excavated a mound of sod
in such excess to inter
there could be no hope for God
to manifest
an earthly return.

But that was not to be
for here's the mystery:
The miracle of wine, fishes, and loaves
were tangibles that we could see.
But who can see a buried heart
rising?

Vessel

Expression

oozes

out

of me.

Observe

how the Maker

wrought me.

Explore my curves.

Run your fingers across my lip.

Dip into my dark cavity.

Caress my round bottom.

Am I warm

or does a chill surge through you?

At times, life pours from me –

other times, I hold death.

Draped in blossoms

I attract your eyes

but do you see my

spheres

of existence?

Is there a heart

beating there?

A soul?

I am within
my Creator.

My Creator
is within me.

Dark, Quiet Rooms

We come into the world
rocked and cradled
in dark, quiet rooms
save a cry,
Touch me! Hold me! Love me!
We come into the world shouting,
Here I am! Look at me!
I am your promise.

We go out of the world
rocked and cradled
in dark, quiet rooms
save a cry,
Touch me! Hold me! Love me!
We go out of the world whispering,
Here I am! Look at me!
Remember me.

Meeting God

At age of five
on the Jersey shore
my playful father
placed me in a rubber tube

to float with him in the ocean.
A huge wave rushed at us
and forced the tube
to break his hold.

I slipped away.

I spilled deep under a wave
plunging down
in the green, grainy sea
gulping and gasping for air –

until I saw a light
beyond my grasp.
In my being, I sensed it was the Lord.
I was calm and unafraid.

Then, in a sudden surge a wave
tossed me onto the sand.
My father held me
as he never had before.

Ever since
I have been reaching for

that promised glimpse of light –
the light of God

through every test
on every shore.

TRIBUTES

He's a kind man
to whom one brings
one's cat with bleeding paw
one's car with dragging muffler
a poem that needs work
a sad story
a favorite broken bowl
a nightmare
an aching heart
the last rose of summer

For Fred Marchant

There's a taste in my mouth for poetry –
for evenings such as last
when you read
in that direct-conversational tone
like you were talking just to me.

You had a playful look
of challenge and humility
as you checked your watch
and looked into our eyes
more curious about those listening
than those listening might have been.

Reaching with your bending frame
as though to grasp us, hold us
take us into you, with you
walk with you
swim with you
ever mindful of the time
and that
the parting must begin.

Arturo Vivante

There's a bit of swagger
where the name
and the man
come together.

Another student, naïve,
ignited by his older charm,
dishevelment.
His air of confidence
and his experience
will try her innocence.

He reads her spark
above the candlelight
and moves in to fan it.

Attraction flickers
as they sip and savor
sweet coffee and cream
bread, butter, and jam.

Sunday Morning

(for Paul)

He traded serving bread and wine
for serving eggs and buttered toast
to hungry babies
drooling
and gurgling in their orange juice.

Instead of choirs singing high
in Latin choruses
Dada, Dada, rings in chants
down the stairs at crack of dawn.

His colored robes
have turned to spotted t-shirts
designed with stains of tears
and running noses.

And sermons, sailing over heads
from a lofty pulpit
now settle breakfast-table squabbles
and family love-concerns.

Boy

In puerile glory
racing forward
tumbling
like clothes in the dryer
faster than the speed of light
Superman
with rumpled hair
smudged chin
eyes that dart
arms spin.

No time to rest
one moment here
there in the next –

Skids to a landing
bumps into walls
soars over railing post
falls
sails down
digs under couch
unearths
treasure chest
of pearls
she thought were lost.

Then triumphantly
with a peck
flings the strand
around his mother's neck.

Speed

I would have told James Dean,
Slow down!
if I'd've been his girlfriend,
and a passenger in his car.

If I'd've been going to that race with him
I'd have said,
Jimmy, you'll have plenty of time
to go fast when you're on the racetrack!
Just go at the speed limit, you hear?
'Cause I want to get there, too,
and be with you.

Jimmy loved me.
He hated to make me mad.
He'd have slowed down.
He'd've made it to that race.
He'd've won
with a trophy in his hands.

He'd have blown me a kiss and smiled,
and then when I ran to him he'd have
thrown his arms around me and said,
Thanks, Judy. I couldn't have done it without you.

Jimmy Dean, oh, Jimmy Dean.
You were only twenty-four
when you sped through death's door.
You needed a girl who cared, like me.

Grandmom

Drinks beers, sheds tears.
Laughs at husband's jokes.
Broke.

Hides rotten teeth
when she eats.

Covers her pain
stooped at the sink.

Can't clear the air
of the dismal stink.

Has another drink.

Desire clings
like mothballs
to her sweaty old clothes

for a man, I was told,
she would never hold.

She always was a Lady

I saw him buck nekkid!
my not truly related
quite antiquated
maiden aunt declared –
the only man, she testified,
she'd ever spied bared.

Though she never told us
who he was,
the way she said it, not unkindly,
still reminds me of her sense of humor
and her laugh.

She was a family mystery –
all we young ones knew about her history:

She sipped sherry on Christmas
sitting in a straight-backed chair
slim ankles crossed modestly
fingers lightly smoothing down her hair.

The scent of lavender cologne settled
on the surface of her thin
powdered-white, translucent skin.

She was so afraid of thunder
she hid in closets
during storms,
and she worked at Kresge's
all her life,
sewing on dressmakers' forms.

Her father was
a Yankee soldier
in the Civil War
(I have his letter from the trenches
to his mother by my door).
Her ma, in Sussex, had a farm
where they found her dead.
She helped Nana with the housework,
washing linens, baking bread.

She had no living relatives
save her borrowed kin,
but rumor has it, say the cousins,
that our Grandpop
with his philanthropic charm
for more than Christian charity,
took Aunt Florence in.

In Serried Lines

I am standing on the shoulders
of my ancestors.
They have formed the foundation
for my evolution.
All the women,
back through my family line,
have brought me to this age,
this life, this time.

Great-great grandmothers, to grandmothers,
then to my mother, walk with me
as I pass their lifeblood to my daughter,
granddaughters, their daughters,
until there are no daughters.

I don't forget the fathers.
But the teaching, tenderness, traits, and tales
those women planted in my soul
now flow through me to flower in my spirit.

And the essence of my being,
my longings, my beliefs,
sprung from the soil of my past,
I will hand down to my kin
so humankind may live in harmony.
Bringing us together
as we walk in serried lines.

Cycles

We are the daughters of the mothers
and the mothers of the daughters –
sisters forevermore.

We pass through the cycles
as the cycles pass through us
and the many moons unite us
in this never-ending sphere.

And our mothers we remember
as the orbs around us shining
when they are just the little girls
in grown-up mothers' clothes.

It's the daughters
with their trusting eyes
who give us all the mother-sense
a disbelief that they are ours
not really ours
transmits the motherlove to them.

There is no way to tell a mother
surely truly tell a mother
about the small comforts
we never can forget.

But a mother knows her daughter-mother
knows by caring for her daughter
and the chain will link those endless loves
unto eternity
encircling all the daughters
and their mothers.

Tribute to My Mother

As a child raised on Dad's low income,
my mother's tuna casseroles
were often served – especially during Lent.

My fondness for those casseroles
I attribute
to my creative mother.

I like the challenge of "nothing"
left in the refrigerator
to pique my interest.

I find bits of onion, dried up mushrooms,
soggy celery, a lingering clove of garlic,
container of condensed soup, left-over green beans,

saltines, a wedge of butter, broth
made from the seeds and stalks of vegetables
or roasted chicken bones,

a can of tuna skulking
behind baked beans on the shelf
and opened packages of noodles.

With some sautéing, seasoning, and baking
the concoction
arrives

on the table lit with candles,
adorned with gleaming goblets,
cloth napkins in their rings,

to be scooped
onto spotless plates.
And the final touch,

a nod to Mother's flair to meet
my father's taste for something sweet,
a dollop of grape jelly on the side.

Memorial Day Dessert

Dad
telling war stories
pushing back from the table
full, relaxed, youthful
though grey streaks invade his hair.

Remembering fellow Marines
bombed
just as he left the gully
to get more ammunition.

War stories for dessert
from my purple-hearted Dad.

How close he came
to a flag and a grave
in place of coffee and a piece of cake.

Magnolias

or a bouquet of violets.
I'd bring them on my knees.
I'd kiss those thin cheeks,
and veined hands,
I've inherited from you,
dear Mother.

Your eyes gray, confused
haunt me from that day
before I understood,
or could accept
you were leaving.

Could they
with a flash of bright light
lift out of their dark wells
from pain I caused
when I lashed out
at your fading memory

hearing you repeat
the same question
over and over?

Will you forgive me?
Will you forgive me?
Will you forgive me?

About My Father

This is about my father
but it could be about any father
maybe even yours.

I will speak as if I do not remember
the scent of tobacco on his shirt
when he held me
on his lap
when I was sad
or when this gruff man
would carefully collect
my falling tears
or that I felt so safe
when I was at his side
when there was something to fear
because I want it to be
about your father, too.

He would not want me to mention
his stroke
and infirmities
before his overdose
and subsequent demise
because he was strong
and proud
and embarrassed that he fell down
when he tried to walk
and that he had to be changed
and he couldn't say the words
he wanted to say.

I won't say those things
because it wouldn't be
about your father, too.
But it could be.

Full Plumage

Womanliness flows from her pores
from the curve of her elbow
where babies slept
from the swell of her groin
where hungry men urged her on
from areolas tipping mounds
of powdered breasts.

Perfume rises out of her
in waves from a secret spring
scenting the air when she appears
trailing its aroma when she leaves.

They have called her beautiful
and made her beautiful because of it.
She is careless with her caresses.
All those she encounters
feel the surge of her love.

She is an enchantress who charms
the wary and afraid –
even the wise and disillusioned –
with a magnetic force none can resist.

Her almond-shaped eyes see into the future
her slim fingers turn pages of the past
but she lives in the present
with gratitude for all her gifts.

She has fulfilled the promise of girlhood
the requirements of motherhood

the tests of marriage, divorce, and life alone.
In what might be called her elder years
she's achieved full plumage.

To Stanley Kunitz

Would you allow this poor poet
to cast her shadow upon your door?
For poetry or eternity
your signature in her book
would be a sage's hand
against her brow.

Acknowledgments

A Sense of Place, An Anthology of Cape Women Writers, Ed. Anne Garton, 2003: Anthology, Motherhood, Siren

A Woman's Heart (Judith Partelow) 2014: A Hair's Breadth, A Man Like You, Alone Together, Apron #1 & #2, Arturo Vivante, Bedtime Story, Between Us, Breasts, Dirty Linen, Encounter, Full Plumage, Heart of the Matter, I used to write, Journal Entry, Love's Mystery, Love Quest, Motherhood, Second Chance, Siren, That One, The Comfort of Knowing, Uncommon Sense

Baha'i Anthology on Martyrs, (Shirin Sabri) 1985: Censure

Black Thursday (play by Albert Oubochowsky) 1985: Censure

Cape Cod Poetry Review, Volume I, Winter 2012; Editor John Bonanni, Gemma Leghorn; Contributing Editor Gregory Hischak: Fourteen

Cape Cod Times Poetry Section: Parent Night (2019), Tomato Plant (2020)

Cape Women Online, Holiday Issue 2008, Pub. Gillian Drake: The Gift

Carry Me Back, A Woman's Life in Poetry; Scargo Hill Poets, 2018: About My Father, Age, Anthology, Asylum *(Under title: Home Care)*, Captive, Carry Me Back, Faith in Surgical Day Care, Falling Angels, Going Home, Gone, Half-Life, Ironing, Jersey Girl, Last Poem to You, little marriages, Magnolias, Memorial Day Dessert, On My Birthday, Red, Reverie, a.k.a. Reflection, Ritual, Save Me, Scars, She always was a Lady, Sunday Morning, Train Story, Tribute to My Mother, Unwelcome Guest, Vessel, When I Am Dead, Winter's Melody, Young Girls in White Blouses

City of the Covenant News, June 1985, Pub. Local Spiritual Assembly of the Baha'is of New York City: Censure

Cotuit Center for the Arts, 2011, *"The Dark Side," Open juried exhibition:* Censure

From the Farther Shore, Discovering Cape Cod and the Islands Through Poetry, Published by Bass River Press (imprint of the Cultural Center of Cape

Cod) in collaboration with Calliope: Poetry for Community: WCAI Poetry Sunday, 2021: Cape Cod Life

***Katherine Lee Bates, Falmouth, MA Poetry Contest** - First Place Winner (Adult Category)*, 2013: Asylum

***Lands End: Provincetown's Poets Wax about Love**; Laura Shabott, 2012:* Marry me!

***Mutual Muses, Cotuit Center for the Arts**, 2023:* Remembrance, Mariupol Hotel

Mutual Muses, Cultural Center of Cape Cod: Reverie, One Summer's Day, Hoeing, Save Me, Crazy Horse

***Slant Magazine, A Journal of Poetry**; Summer 2018:* Recycled

***Soul-Lit, On-Line Journal of Spiritual Poetry**; Summer Issue 2020*; Editor Wayne-Daniel Berard: Moments (for Reflection)

***Spiritual Mothering Journal**, Dover, NH, 1985:* Cycles

***Veterans' Poetry for Peace** (second place winner, 2013):* Going Home

***Voices from A Borrowed Garden, A Collection of Poetry**, D.L. Hermann, Ed., 1990, Louhelen Baha'i School Council:* I used to write

***WOMR Outermost Poetry Contest**, Marge Piercy, Judge 2013, (2nd place regional winner), Bedtime story; 2021 (Honorable Mention):* Summer's Harvest

***World of Water, World of Sand, A Cape Cod Collection of Poetry**, Fiction and Memoir, Compiled and Edited by June Beisch, Gillian Drake and Virginia Reiser, Cape Cod Literary Press, 2006:* Clear Eyes, Half-Life

Thanks to the Scargo Hill Poets where many of the poems herein were workshopped and improved with their critiques. I am most appreciative of the Cape Cod Writers Center, the nonprofit organization that has helped to inspire and educate so many writers in all facets of publication. Thank you to my many friends and relatives who have been supportive and encouraging over the years! You are so appreciated, believe me. Thanks to Atmosphere Press for helping to get this publication realized.

Most especially, thank you to my children for your love and support. I know it's difficult to see your mother's thoughts and life in poetry splashed across the pages for all to see. The father of my children makes appearances here, as well he should in our long history together. My second husband influenced many of the poems. And Thom Slayter deserves accolades for his patience, encouragement, and all the love anyone could possibly give as a friend, lover, and husband. Together these and others figure into my life's journey in poetry. I am deeply grateful for all the inspiration they've given me.

About the Author

JUDITH PARTELOW is a playwright, journalist, reviewer, theatre/ film actress, director and former teacher of drama and English. As a professional actress, she has also read and recorded poetry of Toby Olson and all of Richard Wainwright's children's books. She created two chapbooks of her work: *A Woman's Heart* and *Carry Me Back, A Woman's Life in Poetry*. She's developed a play from her poetry, also entitled *A Woman's Heart*, and in collaboration with others, another play called *NEIGHBORS!* addressing racism. She is featured in several cable TV interviews and poetry readings online. She lives on Cape Cod with her husband, Thom Slayter.